The Red Box

Written by Elizabeth Sengel

STECK-VAUGHN
COMPANY

A Division of Harcourt Brace & Company

Mom has a red box. She keeps it under her bed. "What's in that box, Mom?" I asked.

2

Mom smiled. She didn't tell me. She just gave me a hug and said, "Let's get ready."

I got ready for my big game. I put on my cap and got my bat. I forgot all about the red box.

4

Mom yelled as I went up to bat. I hit the ball. Wham! I ran and ran. It was a home run!

That night I saw Mom in her room. She had the red box on her lap.

"Mom, what's in that box?" I asked.

Mom just smiled and said, "It's time for bed."

The next day Mom and I made a lot of sandwiches. We put them in a basket. We got a bag of apples, too.

We put the lunch in the van. Then we picked up the rest of the team. We went on a picnic. I forgot all about the red box.

At home that night, I got a book. I wanted to read it to Mom. I saw that red box again!

"What's in that box, Mom?" I asked. Mom just smiled and patted the lid.

The next day Mom and I planted flowers. We had fun putting them into pots. I patted the dirt.

Mom added water to each pot. I set the pots on the window sill. Mom and I did a good job.

That night Mom and I put a puzzle together. The puzzle box made me think about Mom's red box. "Mom, what's in your red box?" I asked.

Then Mom showed me. There were so many things in that box! There was one of my old caps. There were my rocks. There was my old toy truck.

15

"I am saving bits of you," Mom said.

"Why?" I asked.

"Because I love you," Mom said.

16